Caterpillars to Butterflies

Inspiration to Become Your Best Self

BOOK OF POETRY

CAROLYN KYLE

Copyright © 2019 Carolyn Kyle
All rights reserved
First Edition

PAGE PUBLISHING, INC.
New York, NY

First originally published by Page Publishing, Inc. 2019

ISBN 978-1-68456-546-7 (Paperback)
ISBN 978-1-68456-548-1 (Hardcover)
ISBN 978-1-68456-547-4 (Digital)

Printed in the United States of America

We delight in the beauty of the butterfly, but rarely admit
the changes it has gone through to achieve that beauty.
—Maya Angelou

This book is dedicated to my two sons, Giovanni and Darren Jr.

You have been an inspiration to me throughout my journey called life. Because of you, I have learned to persevere and stay strong through many hard and challenging situations. I pray that my faith and strength have been an example to you that you may conquer whatever challenges life may bring along the way. I hope that you will never allow anything or anyone to deter you from your purpose, use every opposition as a stepping-stone. I love you and pray that I have done my job as your mother and thank you for being such loving children.

Love you always,
Mom

Contents

Definitions 9

Butterflies 11
Transform 12
A New Day 13
Up 14
The Fall 15
Peace 16
The Walk 17
Pain to Gain 18
Pride 19
No Change 20
Tomorrow Is Today 21
The Beauty Inside 22
Hidden Treasure 23
Refreshed 24
The Gift 25
Keep It 100 26
The Race 27
The Evolution 28
Original 29
Something Bigger 30
Elevate 31
In Pursuit 32
Intercede 33
Do Something 34

Transition	35
Fear	36
Time and Season	37
Faith	38
God's Love	39
Overcomer	40
Time	41
Intended	42
Say Something	43
The Word	44
Be Honest	45
Ready to Heal	46
Let It Slide	47
Oppressed	48
Too Short	49
Be Free	50
The Cover-Up	51
Don't Expect	52
Hidden	53
Human	54
Hurt	55
I Am	56
Trust	57
Words	58

Definitions

Metamorphosis: A complete change of character, appearance, or condition.

Become: To evolve, change into, or emerge as something.

Best: Of the highest quality, to the greatest degree, in the most effective way.

Butterflies

It is not at all what it seems
As a matter of fact, it's ugly
But that's just the first step
Transition must happen to be the best
The process begins at ground level
But the end result is extra special
Everything with purpose has a season
In time it's revealed for a reason
Butterflies are beautiful in the end
Change must happen to transcend

Transform

The mind is a terrible thing to waste
It has power, so why do we hesitate
To search for knowledge
Like a freshman in college
It gives you a new direction
The ability to change and make corrections
Everything with beauty must be transformed, you see
Like a caterpillar in a cocoon planted on a tree
When the time has fully come, a butterfly will emerge
So renew your mind and take heed to what you've heard

A New Day

A new day that is covered in grace
Filled with mercy, come what may
Life and death are in my tongue
Speaking victory, I've already won
Making life changes along the way
Feeling growing pains day to day
All things are working for my good
Yes, even the bad I knew it would
He knows my ending from the start
If I trust Him, He'll do His part
A closer relationship now I seek
So I may hear clearly when He speaks
I was predestined to do His will
And with my life, I will fulfill
When I'm confused, can't find my way
I look to Him and seek His face

Up

Up, up, and away
Up is where I plan to stay
There high above the clouds
And no man can bring me down
Far away where no skies are gray
Reaching for greatness every day
On my way up, I won't look down
Never let my feet touch the ground
Stepping out on faith will be the key
The only thing stopping me is me
On another level, I will soon be
If I trust God and just believe

The Fall

Pride comes before a fall
That pertains to us all
Don't let time slip away
Waiting for another day
Doesn't matter who's right or wrong
Don't waste time trying to be strong
All because you want to save face
Humble yourself and He'll give grace
Admittance is the main key
To open up and be set free
Self-denial is a heavy load
Forgive yourself and let it go

Peace

It soothes you when all seems lost
Sometimes it will cost
Everything you thought was good
It is often misunderstood
You see, there's a peace that can't be explained
When you give up things that were gained in vain
Like the calm after a raging storm
The feeling you have when you are reborn
A fresh outlook through brand-new eyes you see
What you could have if you'd let go and just believe
In the One who gave you another chance
To get it right because your life is in His hands

The Walk

Inch by inch is where we all begin
We stumble; we crawl
Yes, sometimes even fall
Holding on for dear life
But determined to fight
To overcome the fear inside
We take one step at a time
Eventually standing on our own two feet
But as we walk down the line
We finally realize
He was there all the time

Pain to Gain

Muscles are built through resistance
That's only if we can go the distance
Tolerating the pain along the way
In order to make them strong
We can no longer prolong
The work that it will take
But if you never move
How can you improve
And get good results if you may
Stay focused
There is no hocus-pocus
Just hard work
After all, Rome wasn't built in a day
It's the price we must be willing to pay

Pride

What keeps us from our fate
One thing that the Lord hates
It causes division and frustrates
Obedience to Christ in the worst way
Pride comes before a fall
So we won't answer His call
That would line up and regulate
God's purpose for His people today
Therefore, I would like to advise
Here's one word to the wise
Humble yourselves every day
Get down on your knees and pray
That you may stand and keep the faith
Allow Him to lead you all the way

No Change

People want to lose weight
But how many times have you ate
No change
No luck when looking for a mate
But not willing to meet them halfway
No change
Tired of working hard for low pay
But won't get out the box to elevate
No change
Disgusted with life depressed always
But won't do anything but complain
No change
Things will always remain the same
Until you decide to make a change

Tomorrow Is Today

I often wonder why
Life seemingly passes by
Could it be we always rely
On tomorrow to give it a try
Making decisions along the way
Creating issues from day to day
Though old habits are hard to break
Compromise requires a little give-and-take
To get the most of what we proclaim
Change must come, or stagnant we'll remain
So never put off for tomorrow
What should be done today

The Beauty Inside

Beauty is only skin-deep
You need wisdom to be complete
Gain some knowledge along the way
It is a must in this world today
Who you are is not epitomized
By your hips, your hair, or your eyes
You were purposed for more than this
Have integrity; add that to your list
A woman's worth can't be denied
But you must know you are the prize
Faith in the One who knows you best
Will get you there if you pass the test

Hidden Treasure

More than diamonds and pearls
Wisdom and knowledge are supreme
Its power waiting to transcend
Worth more than you can imagine
Not given to many men
When found, it is indeed a pleasure
It is that of a hidden treasure
To cherish like that of gold
Its riches and wealth are untold

Refreshed

My thoughts had me so confused
I asked God what I should do
To uplift this heavy load
Before my heart turned bitter and cold
Walking in love to no avail
Sometimes I felt my life I failed
Until one day His power overwhelmed
Down on my knees, to the floor I fell
He reminded me of what He said
And refreshed my spirit once again

The Gift

Let it go
Let it flow
Gotta keep moving
Constantly improving
Like the sound of a symphony
Playing in perfect harmony
To whom much is given
Much is required
Now it is my desire
To reach and inspire
Dig down deep
And go a little higher
Displaying my gifts
That I may uplift
All whom I encounter
Because of the One
Who has all power

Keep It 100

Don't be afraid to be who you really are
That means with all your bruises and scars
There are no perfect people, you see
But there is one just for you and me
Why pretend to be something you are not
After all, that's not realistic or very smart
What's on the inside will eventually come out
And what once was good, people will begin to doubt
So always keep it 100; it is a must
Because if you don't, there will be no trust

The Race

All I have is my faith
Although my blessing is on the way
Sometimes it's hard while I wait
Because I feel they are delayed
So I pray to God each and every day
To give me strength along the way
But how much longer will it take
'Cause I don't think I can make it
The race is given not to the swift or strong
But to the one who endures through it all
Then I heard a small voice say
"Don't be anxious, you can take it
Because where you are today
Will surely pass if you keep the faith"

The Evolution

Always evolving
Constantly resolving
Making drastic moves
I won't stop
Revolutionary
Never customary
Taking steps to improve
On my way to the top

Original

Why do you feel the need to be
Accepted in society
Conforming to the world you see
Only leads to destruction ultimately
If you renew your mind
Transformation you will find
An original by design
The only one of its kind
Created with purpose and authenticity

Something Bigger

There is something deep down within
And it's taunting me like a whirlwind
Something bigger than I can see
It's living somewhere inside of me
The feeling of greatness
A perpetual heaviness
It gets stronger day by day
Like a butterfly in a cocoon
It takes over me and consumes
Because my destiny is on the way

Elevate

Why do I allow things to escalate
When He has already made a way of escape
Therefore, I get to choose my fate
Taking the high road
It means I have total control
Of what will go down and unfold
Walking proudly up the ladder
I won't cry over spilled milk
It doesn't really matter
No, I don't have to perpetuate
I simply choose to elevate

In Pursuit

Always pursuing
Always renewing
His love for me
Even though I keep moving
Away from Him
But on who else can I depend
To build me up
Fill my cup
Give me a second chance
Because He can enhance
Every area of my life
So in Him I will delight
Because He paid the ultimate price

Intercede

Intercession is necessary
When battling the adversary
Standing in behalf of another
It may be your sister or brother
Tearing down the walls of iniquity
Destroying the weapons of the enemy
Wrestling not against flesh and blood
For this war Christ has already won

Do Something

Faith without work is dead
Can't people get that through their head
Always believe in every word He said
But actions must take place instead
Of waiting, anticipating on a wing and a prayer
Don't work, don't eat, and your cupboard is bare
All because you never moved took a leap or prepared
Yes, timing is a must, I do declare
Seedtime and harvest, but in the meantime, work is fair
To get what He has for you
Standing still just won't do

Transition

I'm on a mission
To get in position
Like a sprinter on his mark
A new beginning I will start
I trust and never doubt
What life is really about
Purpose, growth, and change
I don't aspire to stay the same
Like a cocoon, I'm in transition
Putting in work I am commissioned
To make an impact
On this cold, brutal world today

Fear

False evidence appearing real
Always in your mind making you feel
As if it will manifest itself
For you, there will be no help
Thoughts racing through your mind
Most often you will find
Are just a figment of your imagination
Insecurity sets in and creates a situation
That will often terrorize, even paralyze
Until your eyes are open and you realize
That it is poison from the enemy
It is put there so you won't succeed
There is nothing to fear but fear itself
So renew your mind and prepare yourself

Time and Season

Everything in life happens for a reason
When it boils down, it's about time and season
Decisions that were made
Even the games that were played
All things working together in the end
To fulfill His purpose once again
Trusting in the one thing that we can depend
His grace and mercy, there is no end
Rebellion has prolonged what He did intend
In the beautiful garden is where it all transcends
Metamorphosis is a process, you see
We must all be transformed from a seed to a tree

Faith

The substance of things hoped for
The evidence of things not seen
We all struggle with that in our lives
Do you know what I mean
Finances, health, and relationships
They all can be
A testament of our faith
If you just trust and believe
So count it all joy
Knowing your reward
Is much greater than what you had before
Perseverance is a must
Only if you trust
In the One who made you from the dust

God's Love

Doesn't matter what the situation
It has no stipulations
Doesn't matter what the cost
Is willing to take a loss
Doesn't harbor any hate
Is willing to cover your mistakes
Doesn't look out for oneself
Is always willing to give help
Unconditional love is what God gives
Because of Him, we now may live
Willing to forgive all our sins
So in the end, we may win

Overcomer

"Never alone" is what the song says
So I don't have to worry
I look ahead instead
Putting what is done behind
Casting down imaginations in my head
I choose to renew my mind
I bury the past; it's dead
More than an overcomer, like thunder
I rise above obstacles, and no man can put me under
For He is the One who cannot lie
So I aspire to reach the sky
Because of He who holds my life
I shall live and never die
And you may ask the reason why
Because with Him I shall reside

Time

This thing, it never stops
Doesn't matter if you're ready or not
It is designed to do just one thing
To keep going in spite of everything
Before you know it, time will slip away
Get it together; don't wait another day
Make the most of what has been given
Prove to them that you are driven
Go ahead; take it to another level
In spite of the traps sent by the devil
The time is now; get to it
Stop procrastinating; just do it

Intended

Oh, say, can you see
How man was truly meant to be
Everything God had intended
From the beginning until the end
He made him first from the dirt
Put him to sleep then made her
Clear instructions were given to them
Nevertheless, the adversary came in
To taint what was pure and so sweet
Because of disobedience, now are we
Ever so selfish and full of pride
God did not intend this for our lives
The enemy will use who he can get
To keep us divided with no regrets
Can two walk together if not agreed
Absolutely not, it can never be

Say Something

Don't just talk; say something
You don't have that right for nothing
Your tongue holds so much power
Don't allow your words to devour
Positive vibes
State of minds
You were given the freedom of speech
Make it count when you speak
Taking for granted the words you say
May cause some harm along the way
So don't just talk to be heard
Make it count, give people a word

The Word

A need, a thought, a word
Manifestation occurred
Powerful words were spoken
Light ignited from the dark
The stars, the moon, the sun
It had only just begun
In the beginning was the Word
Just in case you never heard
How man came to be
He was made from the dust, you see
Everything God made was good
Selfish decisions made it impure
Man's logic and his pride
Caused a curse that now resides
But His love gave us a way out
If we accept it without a doubt

Be Honest

Honesty is the best policy
That's what they say
But how can you be honest
Unless you're in that place
You can't be honest with someone else
Until you've been honest with yourself
Acknowledgment is the key
And that totally depends on me
How can you fix the problem
If you feel there's nothing to solve
Open your eyes so you can see
The solution always begins with me

Ready to Heal

Are we ready to heal
We must first feel
Just keep it real
Going through the motions
Is more than a notion
It leads to destruction
And quite a commotion
People say, what we don't know won't hurt you
But I say, cancer must be addressed
Because it won't simply go away
Are we ready to heal
Before we can build for tomorrow
We must confront what hinders us today

Let It Slide

Let it slide
Let it ride
Don't waste your time
I'm on a mission
Got a lot on my mind
Let it slide
Let it ride
Gotta keep this grind
Need to get my life back
So I can live it sublime

Oppressed

How can this be
For in our minds, we're still in slavery
Battling thoughts of oppression
Keep us in constant regression
Fighting each other
Our own sister and brother
Has kept us in captivity
It affects our progress
So we won't see success
Controlled by pride, greed, and jealousy
Because the facts say the same
Our mentality has kept us enslaved

Too Short

Life is too short
There's something every day
So don't sweat the small stuff
It holds no weight
In one ear and out the other
Don't let it stay
Life is too short
Don't let it slip away
Take a deep breath
Is how to start the day
Life is much too short
Don't have any time to waste

Be Free

If time is of the essence
Then why hold your confession
Speak now or forever hold your peace
Whom the Son sets free is free indeed
That applies to everyone you see
Where there is truth
There is light
Now step out of the darkness
It's a continuous fight
Because it makes no sense
To live each day as a lie
Your tongue holds the power
To dictate your life

The Cover-Up

Never judge a book by its cover
For what's on the inside
Is possibly not what you had in mind
How can this be
It gives a false impression
Not a real expression
Of what resides behind
If you look deep, perhaps you'll find
What they are really trying to hide
A lie that has no room to die
So why the masquerade
The pain won't ever go away
But rather explode like a grenade
Let it go and uncover
What has held you captive and recover
What He has for you today

Don't Expect

If you keep making a mess
Don't expect your house to be clean
If you keep thinking negatively
Don't expect positive results
If you keep spending money
Don't expect to save
If you keep doing the same thing
Don't expect to see anything change
Every seed grows of its kind
So don't be shocked at what you find
It may be too late when you realize
You get back what you sow in life

Hidden

Inside the walls lies past rejection
Sleepless nights with no confessions
All smiles on the outside, it seems perfection
Leaving the voices behind with no regrets
Pushing forward with forgiveness but will never forget
Walking ahead with expectations
Positive thoughts and adaptations
But somewhere in my heart is the hardest part
Letting go of hidden pain
That's where my healing will start

Human

A real live being
We move, think, and breathe
Why do people try to live their lives
As robots with nothing inside
You were made with intelligence
So stop doing things for the hell of it
Emotions are what you feel
C'mon, let's just keep this thing real
Please don't ever try to hide
The pain you feel; just recognize
You are a human being first
And yes, sometimes you're gonna hurt
It's best to be honest with yourself
Instead of living with past regret

Hurt

Hurt people hurt people
That's what they say
But what exactly makes them act this way
Perhaps it's the wall they've set up
In hopes that no one would touch
Or is it the thoughts that come
That make them want to run
How can you see if you are blind
Because you never want to look inside
Down deep is where the pain resides
So why do they constantly try to hide
An open wound will never heal
They're in denial; just keep it real
If they feel you will hurt them again
They will block you so you can't get in

I Am

I am
Beautiful and complex
I am
Intelligent and confident
I am
Strong and sensitive
I am
Powerful and influential
I am
Bold and nurturing
I am
Fierce and understanding
I am
Sassy and creative
I am
Dimensional and independent
I am
Everything God made me to be
I am

Trust

"For I know the plans that I have for you," He declares
But if I believe, why do I keep questioning thee
Always leaning to my own understanding
Trusting not in His capabilities
Trying to keep it together by myself
When I already know He is my help
My faith can't be built on anything else
Struggling to stay afloat
Because I won't let go of what weighs me down in the boat
He says, "Take My hand and together we will stand
Because I have got the master plan
So trust in Me and you will see
Just how good your life was meant to be"

Words

They say sticks and stones
May break your bones
But words will never hurt you
Well, I'm here to say
That it is not that way
Because they often stick and stay
For your words breathe life
So what you say in spite
Will mount up and take flight
If in the moment you are weak
Be careful of what you speak
It's best to be humble and meek
Because once it is said
It can't be taken back; it's not dead
The seeds are planted in their head

About the Author

The author of this book is the youngest of four siblings; she has had years of experience as a leader in the church. Today she has stepped into her calling as an evangelist and decided to use a book as her platform. Everything she has experienced in her life's journey, she wanted to share with others in hopes that it will make them think about why we face challenges in our lives. The author would like to share some godly wisdom that has been imparted into her and impart it into others. Poetry seemed to be a very effective way to get someone's attention and has certainly flowed from her knowledge of the Bible.

    The author lived a life of always encouraging others and thought it would be befitting to write poetry that would uplift and inspire people to become their best selves. Knowing who she is and her purpose has been the main motivating factor in her life, and she hopes to open the eyes of many that change is inevitable, we as people have the choice to allow it to help us grow or to stay stagnant. The author is passionate about helping other's reach their full potential, and she hopes everyone who reads her poems has an intimate look into themselves.

CPSIA information can be obtained
at www.ICGtesting.com
Printed in the USA
LVHW092045240921
698715LV00001B/3